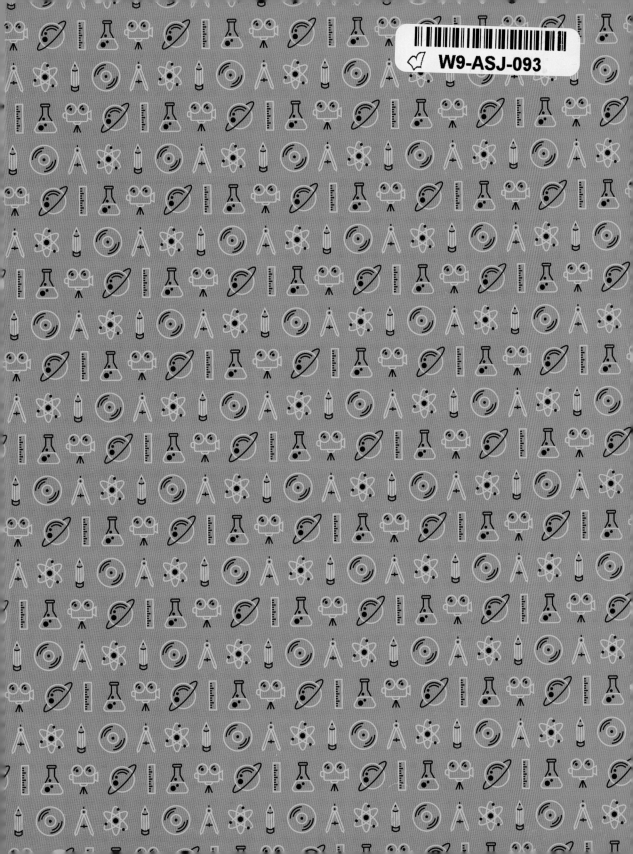

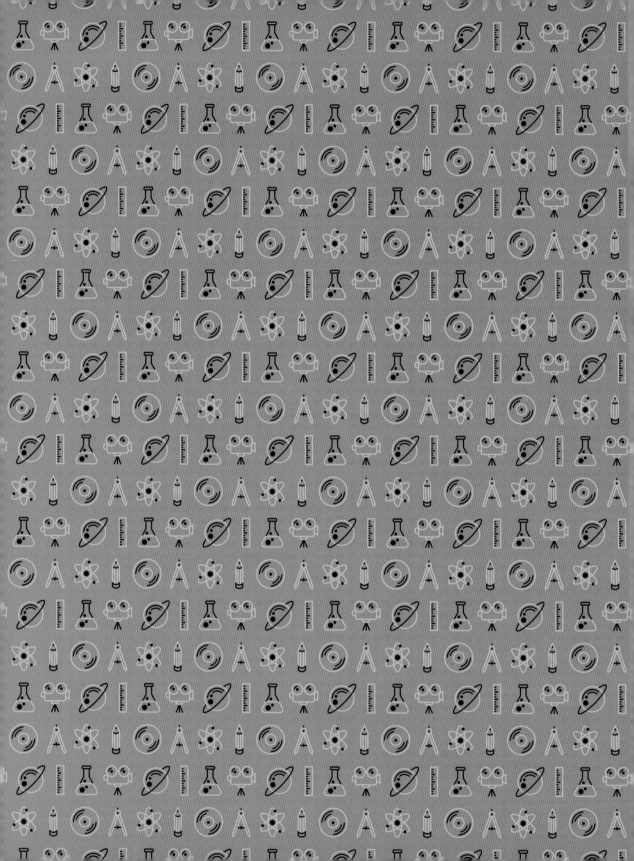

WHO DID IT FIRST?

50 SCIENTISTS, ARTISTS, AND MATHEMATICIANS
WHO REVOLUTIONIZED THE WORLD

Henry Holt and Company, *Publishers since 1866*

Henry Holt® is a registered trademark of Macmillan Publishing Group, LLC

120 Broadway, New York, NY 10271 · mackids.com

Library of Congress Cataloging-in-Publication Data

Names: Leung, Julie, author. | Hart, Alex, editor. | Kuhwald, Caitlin, illustrator.

Title: Who did it first? : 50 scientists, artists, and mathematicians who revolutionized the world /

edited by Alex Hart ; written by Julie Leung ; illustrated by Caitlin Kuhwald.

Description: New York : Henry Holt and Company, [2019] |

Series: Firsts | Audience: Ages 9–12. | Includes bibliographical references.

Identifiers: LCCN 2019002548 | ISBN 9781250211712 (hardcover)

Subjects: LCSH: Biography—Juvenile literature.

Classification: LCC CT107.L5255 2019 | DDC 920.02—dc23

LC record available at https://lccn.loc.gov/2019002548

Our books may be purchased in bulk for promotional, educational, or business use.

Please contact your local bookseller or the Macmillan Corporate and Premium Sales Department

at (800) 221-7945 ext. 5442 or by email at MacmillanSpecialMarkets@macmillan.com.

First edition, 2019 / Designed by Carol Ly

Printed in China by 1010 Printing International Limited, North Point, Hong Kong

1 3 5 7 9 10 8 6 4 2

WHO DID IT
FIRST?

50 SCIENTISTS, ARTISTS, AND MATHEMATICIANS
WHO REVOLUTIONIZED THE WORLD

EDITED BY
ALEX HART

WRITTEN BY
JULIE LEUNG

ILLUSTRATED BY
CAITLIN KUHWALD

HENRY HOLT AND COMPANY · NEW YORK

CONTENTS

INTRODUCTION

Alexa Canady, the first female African American neurosurgeon, once said, "The greatest challenge I faced in becoming a neurosurgeon was believing it was possible."

It takes many years of dedication and hard work to become an important scientist, artist, engineer, or doctor. To achieve a "first," however, takes a willingness to push beyond what seems possible.

The people featured in this book did just that. We'll take a look at fifty pioneers who pushed past the established thinking of their time, past gender and racial barriers, to become a first in the fields of science, technology, engineering, arts, and mathematics.

These great thinkers and visionaries came from all walks of life. Some, like computer scientist Alan Turing, were child prodigies. Others, like John Herrington, the first Native American in space, discovered their calling as adults. You'll meet inventors whose groundbreaking technology revolutionized our modern world and artists whose works have inspired countless others.

It can be a lonely path, being the first. Sometimes, it means waiting for the rest of the world to catch up. You'll meet Ada Lovelace, who wrote the first computer program before modern computers even existed, and the geologist Walter Alvarez, whose theory about dinosaur extinction was mocked for years before it became universally accepted.

Even with so many incredible firsts already accomplished, the world still awaits many more. Who will be the first person to travel to Mars, to construct an artificial mind, or to cure cancer?

We hope these stories inspire you to build on yesterday's achievements, to resist today's boundaries, and to dream beyond what seems possible.

ADA LOVELACE

THE FIRST PERSON TO CREATE A COMPUTER PROGRAM (1843)

> *"If you can't give me poetry, can't you give me poetical science?"*

Growing up, Ada Lovelace was monitored carefully for any signs of misbehavior. That was because her father was none other than Lord Byron, a famed Romantic poet with a bad reputation. Her mother wanted to make sure her daughter would not follow in her father's footsteps, and she put Ada on a strict education of math and science. Nonetheless, young Ada found imaginative ways to apply her scientific learnings. At age twelve, she crafted plans for a personal flying machine, researching materials and studying the wings of birds.

When she was seventeen, Ada met prominent inventor Charles Babbage. At the time, he was in the middle of creating a machine called the Difference Engine. Babbage envisioned a device, composed of gears and cogs, that could process high-level computations. In other words, Babbage was working on the world's first computer.

Ada was fascinated, and the two struck up a lifelong friendship and collaboration. When Charles began work on an even more complex Analytical Engine, Ada could see the machine's potential uses beyond number crunching. Ada was the first to theorize that computing machines could be used to process all sorts of information—including music and art.

Ada set about writing down a sequence of instructions that Babbage's machine could eventually run, called an algorithm. And for that work, she is known as the world's first computer programmer. Babbage never finished building his Analytical Engine, and Ada was unable to test her theories in her lifetime. However, Ada's grand vision for computers proved quite true in time.

MARIA MITCHELL

THE FIRST FEMALE PROFESSOR OF ASTRONOMY
IN THE UNITED STATES (1865)

"

We especially need imagination in science. It is not all mathematics, nor all logic, but it is somewhat beauty and poetry.

"

Maria Mitchell was born into a large family of Quakers who valued education for girls just as much as for boys. Maria's father taught her astronomy in their Nantucket, Massachusetts, home using his personal telescope. At age twelve, she helped him calculate the exact position of their home using a solar eclipse. By age fourteen, she was assisting Nantucket's sailors with their navigational computations, which were vital in helping them find their way home from long whaling journeys. As an adult, Maria studied the sky every clear night, tracking stars and planets.

On October 1, 1847, Maria left a party at her parents' house to visit the rooftop observatory she and her father had built above a bank. When she peered through her telescope, Maria spotted a small and blurry object, just above the North Star, that did not appear on her charts. After confirming with her father, she realized she had discovered her first comet, later called Miss Mitchell's Comet after her.

Maria published a notice of her discovery, initially under her father's name. The discovery launched her into new academic circles among astronomers and other scientists. She was even honored with a gold medal by the king of Denmark. Job opportunities followed, and Maria was about to turn her passion for astronomy into a lifelong career. In 1848, she became the first woman to be elected into the American Academy of Arts and Sciences. And in 1865, Maria Mitchell became an astronomy professor at the newly founded Vassar College, making her also the first female astronomy professor in the United States.

EMILY WARREN ROEBLING

THE FIRST PERSON TO CROSS
THE BROOKLYN BRIDGE (1883)

"

I HAVE MORE
BRAINS,
common sense,
AND KNOW-HOW GENERALLY THAN
ANY TWO ENGINEERS
CIVIL OR UNCIVIL
that I have ever met.

"

Emily Warren Roebling perhaps did not intend to help build one of the most famous bridges in the world. Born in 1843 to an esteemed family in Putnam County, New York, Emily received a proper education growing up. For young ladies of her time, this included housekeeping and sewing, in addition to history and algebra.

In 1865, she married a soldier named Washington Roebling. Emily's new father-in-law happened to be John Augustus Roebling, a civil engineer famous for his suspension bridges. He had just finished a design for a bridge connecting Brooklyn to Manhattan. But after an accident, John died before the project could get started. Emily's husband took over the project for his father. Within just a few years, however, bad luck struck him as well. He developed caissons disease, also known as decompression sickness, from his work in one of the underwater structures (caissons) of the bridge, which quickly left him bedridden.

So Emily stepped in. She began researching the technical issues, learning about the strength of the materials being used, and stress-testing structures. She went to the build site every day to relay instructions from her husband. Emily became so good at managing the project that many suspected she actually was the brains behind the bridge.

The construction took fourteen years, and only with Emily's steady hand did it finally reach completion in 1883. Emily would be the first person to cross the iconic bridge that she helped build. When she did, she carried a rooster with her, a symbol of victory and good luck.

NIKOLA TESLA

THE FIRST PERSON TO INVENT THE AC MOTOR (1887)

"

The present is theirs; the future, for which I really worked, is mine.

"

Growing up in the Austro-Hungarian Empire during an unstable period, young Nikola Tesla had much bigger ambitions than following in his father's footsteps in the Orthodox priesthood. Instead, he took after his mother, who invented household appliances when he was a child. In 1884, Nikola immigrated to the United States to become an engineer. After briefly working for Thomas Edison, Nikola decided to create his own company. Eventually, he set up a laboratory in New York City, where he devised a motor that produced alternating electrical currents, or AC.

The electric motor designs of predecessors like Thomas Edison sent currents in a single direction, which could reach only within one mile of their source. Nikola developed a way for his motor to alternate directions periodically, using rotating magnetic fields. This proved to be a safer and more effective way to transmit electricity over longer distances, like along a city's electrical grid.

Nikola's technology first became known to the wider public when his investor, the industrialist George Westinghouse, tasked Nikola with supplying the electrical lighting for the 1893 World's Columbian Exposition in Chicago. It was a smashing success, and afterward, Nikola was hired to design the first hydroelectric power plant at Niagara Falls to run on alternating current. It was used to power the city of Buffalo, New York, by 1896.

Nikola filed more than three hundred patents during his eighty-six years, though his AC motor is his most far-reaching contribution. Today, alternating current is the global standard for nearly all electrical devices.

BARNUM BROWN

THE FIRST PERSON TO DISCOVER *TYRANNOSAURUS REX* (1902)

> "
>
> *Quarry No. 1 contains . . . undetermined bones of a large Carnivorous Dinosaur . . . I have never seen anything like it.*
>
> "

Born in Carbondale, Kansas, Barnum Brown first encountered fossils in the coal mining pits that dotted his hometown. As a child, he collected shells from nearby deposits. The collection grew so large, it overflowed his room, and his mother made him move everything to the laundry room.

When he was older, Barnum put his fascination for the prehistoric to good use, landing a job as an official fossil hunter for the American Museum of Natural History in New York City. The museum funded his attempts to uncover dinosaur bones all around the world.

In 1902, Barnum led an expedition to the Hell Creek Formation in the rugged mountains of Montana. There, embedded in a rocky cliffside, were the bones of an entirely new kind of dinosaur—one with fearsome teeth and a giant skull. Using dynamite and then horses to pull away the rocks, Barnum and his crew excavated the skeleton and shipped it back to the museum by horse and train. The museum named Barnum's find "the king of tyrant lizards"—better known as the *Tyrannosaurus rex*.

Barnum's discovery of the *T. rex* was just another highlight in a fabled career. His work on behalf of the museum led him to some of the most dangerous regions of the world. Sometimes, the only way his colleagues knew he was still alive was when shipments of fossils, postmarked from faraway places, would suddenly show up on their doorstep. Barnum contributed to so many displays at the American Museum of Natural History, he earned the nickname Mr. Bones.

NETTIE STEVENS

THE FIRST PERSON TO DISCOVER THE SEX CHROMOSOMES (1905)

"

To the question of how sex is determined in the egg, no thoroughly convincing answer has yet been given.

"

Coming of age shortly after the American Civil War, at a time when few girls were educated, Nettie Stevens was lucky to be able to complete a high school–level education. She was a brilliant student, noticed by her teachers and always at the top of her class. Unfortunately, women had limited career options at the time—even the brilliant ones.

After graduating, Nettie became a schoolteacher, but it was only the means to a bigger dream: to be a scientist. She saved enough money to go to Stanford University at the age of thirty-five. Four years later, her dream came true when she became a research scientist, studying genes and how characteristics are passed from parents to children.

Nettie wanted to understand what determines whether someone is born a boy or a girl. She began by examining the cells of mealworms under a microscope and made an interesting discovery. While both female and male mealworms had twenty chromosomes, the twentieth chromosome on the males was significantly smaller. Nettie had just discovered the X and Y chromosomes, which determine sex. From there, she figured out that it had to be the male that contributes the sex-determining chromosome (X or Y) to the offspring, since females can pass on only an X chromosome.

While other scientists made similar discoveries around the same time and some even built upon her research, Nettie's conclusions proved to be the most accurate. She was not given proper credit for her work in her lifetime, and is only now being recognized for the trailblazer she was.

ROBERT H. GODDARD

THE FIRST PERSON TO LAUNCH
A LIQUID-PROPELLED ROCKET (1926)

"

THE DREAM
OF YESTERDAY
is the hope of today
AND THE
REALITY
of tomorrow.

"

Robert H. Goddard was a sickly child, and he was often kept home from school because his mother feared for his health. To pass the time, he read science-fiction novels like H. G. Wells's *The War of the Worlds*. This particular story, about a Martian invasion of Earth, sparked Robert's imagination. He wanted to go to outer space, and he knew he would need a machine to get there.

Because of how much school he missed, he fell behind kids his own age. He was twenty-one when he graduated from high school, but Robert did not let this disadvantage slow him down. He graduated with honors, went to college, and became a physics professor, conducting rocket experiments on the side.

In the beginning, Robert had a hard time getting money for his projects, as many believed his goal of space travel was impossible. At long last, in 1916, he received a small grant from the Smithsonian Institution that allowed him to continue his experiments. Robert tested many rocket models and theories over the next decade, refusing to call any failed attempts "failures," merely "valuable negative information." Finally, on March 16, 1926, he launched a rocket fueled by gasoline and liquid oxygen. It rose 41 feet and landed 184 feet away in 2.5 seconds. It was the first of its kind.

Robert's determination to realize a childhood dream paved the way for our modern rockets today.

MERET OPPENHEIM

THE FIRST WOMAN TO HAVE HER ART PURCHASED
BY THE MUSEUM OF MODERN ART (1936)

Growing up in Switzerland in the 1920s, Meret Oppenheim was surrounded by artistic and intellectual family members. Her grandmother was an author, and active in the women's rights movement. Her aunt encouraged her to collect art prints. Meret, too, wanted to be an independent, creative spirit.

When Meret turned eighteen, she went to Paris to study art. There, she befriended artists in the surrealist movement—a popular approach to art in the 1930s that drew inspiration from the subconscious mind, from dreams and random thoughts.

One day in 1936, Meret was having tea with fellow artists Pablo Picasso and Dora Maar. Pablo noticed Meret's bracelet, which she had made by wrapping a piece of wire with fur. He joked that pretty much anything could be covered with fur. All three began to point to objects that could be wrapped, and Meret suggested her teacup.

Later on, Meret acted on that idea. She bought a teacup, a saucer, and a spoon from a department store in Paris and wrapped them in the pelt of a Chinese gazelle. It was named *Lunch in Fur*, and the piece became an instant icon of twentieth-century art. Alfred H. Barr Jr., the director of New York's Museum of Modern Art, bought it for the museum immediately, making it the first work by a woman that MoMA ever exhibited.

Meret worked in various mediums throughout her life, producing sculptures, poetry, and performance art. In a time when women had a hard time breaking into the art world, she boldly created works that questioned the systems that held women back.

"

Nobody will GIVE YOU FREEDOM;

YOU
have to
TAKE IT.

,,

—MERET OPPENHEIM

MARY GOLDA ROSS

THE FIRST FEMALE ENGINEER FOR LOCKHEED (1942)

"

My state-of-the-art tools were a slide rule and a Friden computer.

"

Born in Oklahoma in 1908, Mary Golda Ross grew up deeply proud of her heritage. Her great-great-grandfather John Ross was the longest-serving chief of the Cherokee Nation. Her great-great-grandmother had died on the Trail of Tears, when Native Americans were forcibly relocated from their homes in the southeastern United States and onto reservations.

Armed with a deep respect for her past, Mary pushed forward. She completed high school at the age of sixteen and first worked as a statistics clerk for the Bureau of Indian Affairs. Still, Mary wanted to aim higher. Before long, she had earned a master's degree in mathematics from the University of Northern Colorado. After discovering an interest in the stars, she also took every astronomy class available to her.

With the US entering into World War II, Mary took a job as a mathematician at Lockheed, the famed aerospace company. There, she and her team worked tirelessly on adding speed and durability to US military aircraft.

Mary then became one of the first engineers at Lockheed's famous Skunk Works, the top-secret program that produced groundbreaking planes like the SR-71 Blackbird jet, which was capable of flying more than three times the speed of sound. Out of forty people, she was the only woman on the team and the only Native American.

Mary would go on to help NASA prepare for its moon landing and other types of space travel. In fact, she was one of the authors of the NASA Planetary Flight Handbook. One hundred thirty years after her great-great-grandfather guided his people on the Trail of Tears, Mary helped guide her country to the stars.

CLAUDE SHANNON

THE FIRST PERSON TO MEASURE DIGITAL INFORMATION (1948)

"

I think the history of science has shown that valuable consequences often proliferate from simple curiosity.

"

Claude Shannon loved to tinker. Growing up in Gaylord, Michigan, he built Erector sets, radios, even an elevator in his barn. At a time when telephone lines had not yet reached rural America, Claude constructed a homemade line so that he could speak to his friends. Naturally, he pursued a career in engineering and mathematics when he grew up.

In 1936, Claude helped build an early computer at the Massachusetts Institute of Technology. From there, he was hired at Bell Labs, where he assisted in wartime efforts to break Nazi codes during World War II. The study of cryptography and computers had a big effect on Claude's ideas on how information could be transferred from one place to another. After the war, he wrote his most important work, "A Mathematical Theory of Communication."

In this paper, Claude proposed that all information could be digitized into ones and zeros, which he called *bits*. This way, the information could easily be sent from one place to another (for example, from one computer to another), intact and uninterrupted. Today, bits are the fundamental unit of size used when referring to digital information. For example, the art on the preceding page is 789,600 bits.

Claude's ideas ushered in a new age of technology, and he is considered the father of information theory. You can thank him for every computer file you've ever opened and every web page you've ever loaded on the internet.

Despite all these groundbreaking accomplishments, Claude never lost his love for tinkering. In his spare time, he built a juggling robot and flame-throwing trumpets!

MARIA TALLCHIEF

THE FIRST PRIMA BALLERINA OF THE NEW YORK CITY BALLET (1949)

"

If anything at all,

PERFECTION

IS NOT WHEN THERE IS

nothing to add,

BUT WHEN THERE

IS NOTHING LEFT TO

take away.

"

Known as Elizabeth "Betty" Marie to her friends and family, Maria Tallchief was born on an Indian reservation in Oklahoma in 1925. Her father was a member of the Osage Nation. Her mother, of Scotch-Irish descent, had grown up poor and was never able to pursue the performance career that she had wanted. So at the age of three, Maria was placed in ballet and piano lessons. When she was twelve, Maria began training under Bronislava Nijinska, a famous instructor in Los Angeles, who inspired her to pursue a career in ballet.

"I looked at her, and I knew this was what I wanted to do," Maria recalled in an interview.

At age seventeen, Maria moved to New York City and was selected as an understudy in the Ballet Russe de Monte Carlo, a renowned Russian ballet company then touring in the United States. One day, when one of the lead ballerinas dropped out, Maria was called to the stage. Her performances received rave reviews from top critics, who praised her energy and speed.

As her fame grew, many tried to persuade Maria to change her last name, Tallchief, so that people would not discriminate against her. Maria refused and continued to perform under her own name. She even spoke out against the unfair prejudices her fellow Native Americans faced in their own country.

Maria was the first American to dance ballet at a number of famed European stages, including the Paris Opera Ballet and the Bolshoi Theatre. Today, she is considered one of the greatest ballerinas of all time, and America's first major prima ballerina.

ALAN TURING

THE FIRST PERSON TO INTRODUCE THE IDEA
OF ARTIFICIAL INTELLIGENCE (1950)

"

I propose to consider the question 'Can machines think?'

"

When Alan Turing was thirteen years old, he was accepted into a prestigious boarding school in Sherborne, England. Unfortunately, the first day of school coincided with a wide-scale workers' strike across Britain, and transportation systems had ground to a halt. Determined not to miss any class, Alan rode his bicycle unaccompanied for sixty miles from his home in Southampton, stopping only once to stay overnight at an inn.

That singular determination and pursuit of knowledge set the tone for Alan's life. Working doggedly as a code breaker during World War II, Alan was a key player in deciphering the Enigma code that kept Nazi military communications secret.

In 1950, he published a paper titled "Computing Machinery and Intelligence," in which he first introduced the idea that computers contain the potential to be as intelligent as humans—and mimic them as well. He even created a test, called the Imitation Game (later called the Turing test), which would determine said intelligence.

On one side of a computer screen sits a human judge, whose job is to chat with another human and a machine. When the machine's responses can no longer be differentiated from the human's, it will have passed the test. In 2014, a computer program called Eugene Goostman, which simulated a thirteen-year-old boy, did just that.

Today, Alan Turing is known as one of the fathers of artificial intelligence—one of his many recognitions. His insights have greatly shaped how we think about the possibilities of technology.

JAMES E. M. WEST

THE FIRST PERSON TO DEVELOP AND PATENT THE
TECHNOLOGY USED IN 90 PERCENT OF MICROPHONES (1962)

James Edward Maceo West's interest in technology had a shocking start— literally. At eight years old, he was almost electrocuted when plugging a broken radio into an outlet. He was briefly paralyzed during the incident. Instead of scaring him, the shock of voltage intrigued him. He wanted to know how and why it happened. He took apart electrical equipment just to see how it worked. By twelve years old, James was working with an older cousin to install electrical wiring into homes in rural Virginia, where he was raised.

His passion for electrical engineering led him to become a research scientist at Bell Laboratories in 1957. Tasked with researching human hearing, James and his colleague, Gerhard Sessler, found that the microphones they were using in their experiments produced a too-weak signal. Microphones in those days also needed a large, expensive battery in order to operate, and only scientists and radio and TV stations were able to use them regularly.

Seeking a better solution to transmitting sounds via electrical signals, James and Gerhard spent four years developing an electret microphone. (*Electret* means any material that can hold an electric charge for a long period of time.) For their electret, James and Gerhard used Teflon, a plastic-like material. It proved much more durable and sensitive to sound than its carbon predecessors.

Today, their technology is present in 90 percent of microphones, including ones used for hearing aids, cell phones, baby monitors, and computers. In his long career, James developed over 250 patents in acoustic inventions. His work transformed the way we are able to record the world around us.

"

ANYTHING THAT COULD BE OPENED *was in danger.* I HAD THIS NEED TO KNOW WHAT *was inside.*

"

— JAMES E. M. WEST

TURN THE PAGE TO MEET SOME OTHER

INVENTORS

Isaac Newton

THE REFLECTING
TELESCOPE (1668)

RALPH BAER

THE ODYSSEY (1972)

LONNIE G. JOHNSON

THE SUPER SOAKER (1989)

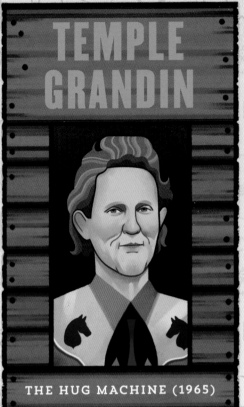

TEMPLE GRANDIN

THE HUG MACHINE (1965)

TIMOTHY BERNERS-LEE
THE WORLD WIDE WEB (1989)

Hedy Lamarr
SPREAD SPECTRUM TECHNOLOGY (1942)

CHARLES FRITTS
THE SOLAR CELL (1883)

THE INVENTORS

ISAAC NEWTON (1642–1727) was an English physicist and mathematician and one of the most influential scientists in history. In addition to proving that light was made up of the colors of the rainbow and creating the mathematical law that proved gravity, his work in the field of optics led to the first reflecting telescope, a telescope in which a mirror is used to collect and focus light, in 1668. This allowed humans to see deeper and more clearly into space.

CHARLES FRITTS (1850–1903) was an American inventor and renowned watchmaker responsible for the first solar cell, an electrical device that converts the energy of sunlight directly into electricity. By coating a sheet of selenium with a thin layer of semitransparent gold, Charles proved the ability to use light as an energy source. Charles's innovative discovery in 1883 was imperative in the development of the technology we use today in solar panels.

HEDY LAMARR (1914–2000) was an Austrian American film actress and inventor. Considered by many the most beautiful woman in film of her day, she kept scientific equipment for experiments in her trailer while working on film sets. With George Anthiel, Hedy patented technology in 1942 that scrambled radio frequencies so messages directing US torpedoes wouldn't be intercepted by Nazis. Better known as "spread spectrum" technology, their invention helped form the technology found in today's cell phones, Wi-Fi, GPS, and Bluetooth.

TEMPLE GRANDIN (born 1947) is an American professor, animal scientist, and spokesperson for autism and humane livestock handling. After observing the calming effects of pressurized squeeze chutes—cages used to contain livestock during routine procedures and examinations—Temple began working on a comparable device for hypersensitive humans. She called her invention the "hug machine" (1965), and its therapeutic effects have helped millions.

 RALPH BAER (1922–2014) was a German American engineer, inventor, and video-game developer, widely acknowledged as "the father of video games." In 1966, while working as an engineer for defense contractor Sanders Associates, Ralph started developing a "game box" that would allow people to play games on a television. In 1971, after a Sanders executive invested in the game box, Ralph filed for the first video-game patent. His invention was later given the name "Odyssey" and was recognized as the world's first video-game system (1972). It became a hit, paving the way for companies like Atari, Nintendo, and Sega.

 LONNIE G. JOHNSON (born 1949) is an American inventor and engineer who holds more than 100 patents. Despite years of inventing thermodynamic systems for NASA and the US Air Force, Lonnie is best known for his reinvention of the squirt gun. After witnessing a homemade nozzle in his bathroom sink shoot a formidable stream of water across the room, Lonnie was inspired to invent a pressurized water gun. In 1989, the Super Soaker was born and, incidentally, so were countless epic pool parties. Today, he works on revolutionizing clean energy production.

 TIMOTHY BERNERS-LEE (born 1955) is an English engineer and computer scientist and is credited with inventing the World Wide Web in 1989. By the end of 1990, Tim wrote the code for three fundamental technologies that remain the foundation of our current internet: URI, HTTP, and HTML. He also is responsible for the creation of the very first web page. Thanks to Tim, millions of people around the world can communicate, post, share, create, and game across thousands of miles instantly.

JANE GOODALL

THE FIRST HUMAN TO BE ACCEPTED INTO
A CHIMPANZEE COMMUNITY (1963)

When Jane was one year old, her father gave her a stuffed chimpanzee named Jubilee. Baby Jane adored the toy. Little did the family realize, Jubilee was the beginning of a lifelong devotion to chimpanzees. Throughout her childhood, Jane cared deeply for animals. And above all else, she wanted to be where the most interesting animals were—Africa.

When Jane was twenty-two, an old schoolmate wrote to her from Kenya, inviting her to visit. Jane seized the chance to see Africa at last. While there, she met famed paleontologist Louis Leakey, who gave her the opportunity to study the chimpanzees of the Gombe region, in what is now Tanzania.

With little more than a notebook and binoculars, twenty-six-year-old Jane approached her work differently than most scientists. For example, instead of counting the number of chimpanzees from afar, Jane spent hours and hours just watching in the jungle, waiting for chimpanzees to show up and get comfortable with her presence. Once she watched long enough to learn how to understand and mimic their behaviors, she communicated with them. Her hard work and patience paid off, as the chimpanzees of this area eventually accepted Jane as one of their community.

Jane also gave the animals names instead of numbers and wrote about them as if they were people. Even though some scientists scoffed at this, Jane's writing convinced many people to care about chimpanzees. Today, Jane continues to work tirelessly to preserve the natural habitat of these incredible creatures.

"

It isn't only, HUMAN BEINGS WHO HAVE PERSONALITY,

WHO ARE CAPABLE OF

rational thought [and]

EMOTIONS LIKE JOY

and sorrow.

"

— JANE GOODALL

MARY ALLEN WILKES

THE FIRST PERSON TO DESIGN AND WORK ON A PERSONAL COMPUTER (1964)

> " We worked all kinds of crazy hours and ate all kinds of terrible foods, but we had the best time. "

When Mary Allen Wilkes was in the eighth grade, her geography teacher suggested that she study computer programming one day. In that era, computers were only found in science labs, and Mary had no idea what such a career would look like. It wasn't until she graduated college that she decided to make good on that suggestion.

In the 1950s and '60s, the field of computer science was very welcoming to women. (It became less so by the '80s.) In 1959, Mary began work at the Massachusetts Institute of Technology's Lincoln Laboratory. The Institute was in the process of developing smaller versions of computers, which at the time filled entire rooms. She was tasked with writing a programming language for these LINC computers. LINC computers are now considered the first microcomputers. ("Micro" is generous—the machines were six feet long!)

In 1964, a core group of the scientists moved their work to Washington University in St. Louis, Missouri. Mary didn't want to go, so she continued her work at her parents' home in Baltimore, Maryland. She reconstructed the entire computer in the living room and created an instruction manual for it. Mary was the first person to own and operate a personal computer outside of a laboratory environment! People from the neighborhood would stop by and marvel at Mary's machine.

"My father, who was a clergyman, thought it was absolutely fabulous," Mary has said.

MARY KENNETH KELLER

THE FIRST WOMAN TO EARN A PhD IN COMPUTER
SCIENCE IN THE UNITED STATES (1965)

WE'RE HAVING AN INFORMATION EXPLOSION,

among others, and it's CERTAINLY OBVIOUS THAT

INFORMATION

is of no use unless it's

AVAILABLE.

Not many people would expect that one of the most groundbreaking female computer scientists was a nun, but Sister Mary Kenneth Keller was full of surprises. For starters, not much is known about her childhood or past. We know that Mary was born in Cleveland, Ohio, near the turn of the century. She entered a Roman Catholic order, the Sisters of Charity of the Blessed Virgin Mary, in 1932, and officially joined the order in 1940.

We also know that Mary loved to learn about computers. After obtaining bachelor's and master's degrees from DePaul University, she was accepted at Dartmouth College. (The college had just begun to allow women into its computer center.)

In 1965, Mary became the first woman in the US to earn a PhD in computer science. For her thesis, at the University of Wisconsin, Mary helped develop a computer language called BASIC (Beginner's All-Purpose Symbolic Instruction Code), which made it easier for people to create their own computer software. Before BASIC came along, only mathematicians and scientists could build software. BASIC made coding accessible to a much wider audience. It is still in use today as a way to teach computer programming to beginners.

After receiving her PhD, Mary founded the computer science department at Clarke College in Iowa, which she directed for twenty years. Throughout her life, she was passionate about providing access and information to everyone, not just computer scientists. Mary saw a future where information would "explode" and computers would be instrumental in educating everyone, everywhere—just as it has in the age of the internet.

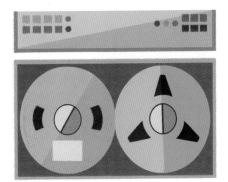

WALTER ALVAREZ

THE FIRST PERSON TO THEORIZE THAT DINOSAURS DIED FROM AN ASTEROID BLAST (1980)

> "Understanding how we decipher a great historical event written in the book of rocks may be as interesting as the event itself."

Walter Alvarez was born into a family with a knack for scientific genius. His father was Luis Alvarez, a famed physicist who, among many achievements, won the Nobel Prize for his work on particle physics. Walter's grandfather and great-grandfather were celebrated physicians. When Walter considered how he might leave his own mark on the world, he decided to become a geologist. As it turns out, his scientific contributions would shed light on the biggest impact on Earth.

One day, Walter made a surprising discovery while studying limestone formations outside a small town in Italy. These rocks can tell a geologist a lot about what conditions were like during prehistoric times. Walter found a thin layer of clay in the limestone, where the fossils of sea creatures that existed in older layers had disappeared.

The distinctive red layer also corresponded with the time period when many of the world's larger dinosaurs died out. Walter called his father, who tested the clay, and found that it was highly enriched in the element iridium. Iridium is very uncommon on Earth but often found in asteroids.

Based on this, Walter and his father theorized that a large asteroid must have struck Earth, causing the extinction of the dinosaurs. Their theory was controversial at first, and for a decade, the theory was met with skepticism and scorn. But as more layers of the same iridium-enriched layers were discovered throughout the world, the Alvarez theory became widely accepted as the truth about what happened to the dinosaurs.

ALEXA CANADY

THE FIRST FEMALE AFRICAN AMERICAN NEUROSURGEON (1981)

Growing up near Lansing, Michigan, in the 1950s, Alexa Canady and her brother were the only black children in their elementary school. Alexa faced discrimination when one teacher gave her lower scores than she actually earned.

Nevertheless, her parents believed that a good education was the key to success. "So what if you're the token black girl. Take that token and spend it," her mother told her.

Alexa took her mother's advice to heart, graduated from high school with honors, and was accepted at the University of Michigan. There, she became interested in medicine during a summer program for minority students. During medical school, she became particularly interested in the complexities of the human brain, and she decided to pursue a career in neurosurgery.

Alexa knew she would face an uphill battle as a woman of color. And in fact, professors often overlooked her questions and disregarded her suggestions. That only made Alexa work harder, reading every publication she could get her hands on and attending every seminar she could.

Finally, she was accepted as a resident at the University of Minnesota's department of neurosurgery, specializing in pediatric care. She'd discovered her true calling in helping the youngest patients. When she finished her residency in 1981, she became the first female African American neurosurgeon in the United States.

Alexa practiced for thirty years before retiring. Looking back, she said among her fondest memories was laughing and playing video games with the children whose lives she saved.

"

The greatest
CHALLENGE
I FACED IN BECOMING A
neurosurgeon
WAS BELIEVING
IT WAS POSSIBLE.
"

—ALEXA CANADY

TURN THE PAGE TO MEET SOME MORE

LEADING LADIES

CAROLINE HERSCHEL

THE FIRST WOMAN TO DISCOVER A COMET (1782)

KATHRYN BIGELOW

THE FIRST WOMAN TO WIN AN ACADEMY AWARD FOR BEST DIRECTOR (2010)

ANTONIA NOVELLO

THE FIRST FEMALE SURGEON GENERAL (1990)

Maria Gaetana Agnesi

THE FIRST FEMALE MATHEMATICS PROFESSOR AT A UNIVERSITY (1748)

DEBBIE GIBSON

THE FIRST WOMAN TO WRITE, PRODUCE, AND RECORD A BILLBOARD NO. 1 SONG (1988)

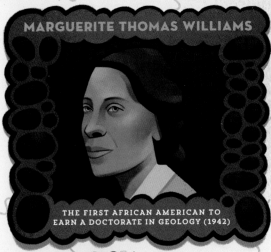

MARGUERITE THOMAS WILLIAMS

THE FIRST AFRICAN AMERICAN TO
EARN A DOCTORATE IN GEOLOGY (1942)

Elizabeth Blackwell

THE FIRST WOMAN TO RECEIVE A
MEDICAL DEGREE IN THE US (1849)

ELLEN SWALLOW RICHARDS

THE FIRST WOMAN ACCEPTED TO MIT (1870)

MEGAN SMITH

THE FIRST FEMALE CHIEF TECHNOLOGY
OFFICER OF THE US (2014)

ELLEN OCHOA

THE FIRST HISPANIC
WOMAN TO GO TO SPACE (1993)

LEADING LADIES

 MARIA GAETANA AGNESI (1718–1799) was an Italian mathematician, philosopher, theologian, and humanitarian. She is recognized as being the first female mathematics professor at a university (1748), as well as the first woman to write and publish a mathematics handbook. Her research in the field of mathematics included some of the earliest discussions of differential and integral calculus.

 CAROLINE HERSCHEL (1750–1848) was a German British astronomer who discovered numerous comets, including her namesake, the periodic 35P/Herschel-Rigollet. Throughout her adult life, she worked alongside her brother William (who discovered the planet Uranus), first in music and then in astronomy. With an orbital period of 155 years, Caroline's comet will next be spotted in 2092 . . . commit the date to memory!

 ELIZABETH BLACKWELL (1821–1910) is recognized as the first woman to receive a medical degree in the United States (1849). She was a pioneer in promoting the education of women in medicine. In 1853, Elizabeth opened a small medical dispensary that was eventually expanded into the New York Infirmary for Indigent Women and Children, an in- and outpatient facility and nursing school run exclusively by women. Today, Elizabeth's infirmary is known as New York-Presbyterian/Lower Manhattan Hospital, one of New York's largest hospitals.

 ELLEN SWALLOW RICHARDS (1842–1911) was an industrial and safety engineer, environmental chemist, and university faculty member who was the first woman accepted to the Massachusetts Institute of Technology (1870), as well as the first female instructor at MIT. In addition to her work in sanitary chemistry, Ellen was a feminist who tirelessly advocated for equal opportunity to education for women.

 MARGUERITE THOMAS WILLIAMS (1895–1991) was an American geologist and geographer. She earned a doctorate in geology from Catholic University of America (1942), making her the first African American to get a

PhD in geology in the United States. In addition to exploring the causes of erosion in the Anacostia River basin, Marguerite was a geography professor at Miners Teachers College in the District of Columbia, a training school for black teachers.

 DEBBIE GIBSON (born 1970) is an American singer-songwriter, record producer, and actress. After writing and recording her own music for years, Debbie's songs found themselves in the hands of a radio personality who shared them with a music executive at Atlantic Records, and the rest is history. In 1988, at the age of seventeen, Debbie's "Foolish Beat" climbed to the top of the Billboard Hot 100 chart, making her the first woman to write, produce, and record a number-one single.

 ANTONIA NOVELLO (born 1944) is an American physician and public health administrator. In 1990, Antonia became the first woman and first Hispanic to serve as surgeon general of the United States, appointed by President George H. W. Bush. During her time as surgeon general, Antonia prioritized her efforts on advocating for the improvement of the health of women, children, and minorities.

 ELLEN OCHOA (born 1958) is an American engineer, former astronaut, and former director of the Johnson Space Center. In 1993, Ellen became the first Hispanic woman to go to space, serving on a nine-day mission aboard the shuttle *Discovery*, whose mission was to study Earth's ozone layer. She eventually flew on three more shuttle flights, two of which went to the International Space Station.

 KATHRYN BIGELOW (born 1951) is an American film director, producer, and screenwriter. Her paintings earned her a spot at the San Francisco Art Institute. She later received a graduate degree in film theory and criticism at Columbia University. In 2010, Kathryn won the Academy Award for Best Director for her film *The Hurt Locker*, making her the first woman to win the prestigious film award.

 MEGAN SMITH (born 1964) is an American entrepreneur who was an executive at Google before becoming the first female chief technology officer of the United States (2014), appointed by President Barack Obama. As CTO, Megan focused on how technology policy, data, and innovation could advance the future of our nation in the digital age.

THAI LEE

THE FIRST KOREAN WOMAN TO GRADUATE FROM
HARVARD BUSINESS SCHOOL (1985)

"

If you focus, if you know what you want and you put together a long-term plan, you can catch up in life, no matter where you are.

"

Though born in Thailand, Thai Lee spent most of her childhood in South Korea. Ever mindful of the tensions between South Korea and North Korea, Thai prepared emergency plans in the event of an invasion. "Whenever we played together, she was always planning our survival," her younger sister has said. "She's the most focused person I've ever met."

That level of preparedness and practicality became a hallmark of Thai's. In her teens, when Thai and her older sister moved to the United States for high school, she focused on math and science, in part because she was self-conscious about her English skills. In college she majored in biology and economics. Thai returned to South Korea and worked to raise enough money to go to business school. In 1983, Thai was accepted to the prestigious Harvard Business School. When she graduated in 1985, she was the first Korean woman to complete the program.

Thai continued her plan for success: learn all about business in her twenties and own a business by her thirties. Thai and her husband at the time bought a failing software reseller called Software House, paying less than $1 million for it. They renamed it Software House International, and Thai grew the business into one of the largest IT providers in the world, with $6 billion in sales!

Even now, despite being a self-made billionaire, Thai does not rely on an assistant. She keeps her own calendar and does her own paperwork. For practical Thai, it wouldn't be a good use of resources. "It would seem wrong to our employees," she said. "And why would I want to waste money like that?"

ARETHA FRANKLIN

THE FIRST WOMAN TO BE INDUCTED INTO THE ROCK & ROLL HALL OF FAME (1987)

"
Music changes, and I'm gonna change right along with it.
"

One Sunday morning at New Bethel Baptist Church in Detroit, Michigan, ten-year-old Aretha Franklin stood up to sing. Her father was the pastor, and gospel music had been a part of her life since birth. Aretha understood that the best singers let emotions power their songs. And when she sang her solo, everyone in the congregation was moved to their feet.

Aretha moved to New York City when she was eighteen years old to pursue a music career. Her career began to take off in 1966, when she signed a deal with Atlantic Records. The company was known at the time for a music genre known as "soul"—a blend of gospel and R & B.

After releasing her first hit single, "I Never Loved a Man (The Way I Love You)," Aretha covered an Otis Redding song called "Respect." She sang the lyrics with so much emotion, "Respect" became an instant hit when it was released in April 1967. Aretha's commanding delivery struck a chord with an entire generation of Americans who were fighting for civil rights and protesting the Vietnam War.

President Barack Obama once said, "American history wells up when Aretha sings." Throughout her long career, she had more than one hundred singles on the Billboard charts and received eighteen Grammy Awards.

In 1987, Aretha was the first woman inducted into the Rock & Roll Hall of Fame, solidifying her status as one of the most powerful voices in music.

SYLVIA
EARLE

THE FIRST WOMAN
TO SERVE AS CHIEF
SCIENTIST OF THE
US NATIONAL OCEANIC
AND ATMOSPHERIC
ADMINISTRATION (1990)

"

EVERY TIME

I slip into the

OCEAN,

it's like going

HOME.

"

When Sylvia Earle was twelve years old, her family moved from New Jersey to Dunedin, Florida. With the Gulf of Mexico right in her backyard, a whole new world opened up. Sylvia received a pair of swimming goggles for her birthday that year. They became a window to explore all the vibrant underwater life up close.

Sylvia wasn't satisfied with snorkeling near the surface. She wanted to dive deeper and stay underwater longer. In college, while studying marine biology and botany, she spent as much time in the water as she could. Everything about the ocean enchanted Sylvia—from giant humpback whales to the microscopic algae that teemed in every spoonful of water. She always wanted to go farther down and discover more.

In 1979, she made an open-ocean dive to the sea floor off the coast of Hawaii, setting an untethered diving record of over 1,250 feet. In 1990, she accomplished another first by accepting an appointment as chief scientist at the National Oceanic and Atmospheric Administration (NOAA)—an organization dedicated to the study of, prediction of change in, and conservation of ocean ecosystems and climates. She was the first woman to hold that position.

Sylvia's greatest goal in life is to help preserve our ecosystems for future generations. She has seen close-up how the ocean suffers at human hands, and she has made tremendous efforts to educate others. "We need the ocean as much as the dolphins, whales, coral reefs, and sea stars do. No ocean, no us," she says.

MAE JEMISON

THE FIRST AFRICAN AMERICAN WOMAN IN SPACE (1992)

"

Being first gives you a responsibility — you have a public platform, and you must choose how to use it.

"

As a kid growing up on the South Side of Chicago, Mae Jemison was obsessed with *Star Trek*. The TV show followed the adventures of crew members onboard an intergalactic starship exploring "space—the final frontier." In addition to the aliens and special effects, young Mae was impressed at how the show depicted different races and genders working together in harmony. Nyota Uhura, played by Nichelle Nichols, the sole African American woman in the cast, became Mae's role model.

When Mae grew up, she took *Star Trek*'s ideals to heart. After attending Stanford at age sixteen, she went on to become an engineer *and* a doctor. She worked in the Peace Corps for two and a half years before applying to join NASA's space program.

In 1992, Mae launched with the space shuttle *Endeavour*, becoming the first African American woman in space. For her trip, she brought along a West African bundu statue, an Alpha Kappa Alpha sorority flag, an autographed poster from famed dancer Judith Jamison, and a picture of Bessie Coleman, the first African American woman to fly a plane. She wanted her culture to be represented in space. In fact, in another nod to her *Star Trek* fandom, Mae began each of her shifts by informing Mission Control Center in Houston: "Hailing frequencies open."

The icing on the cake? In 1993, Mae got a chance to guest star on an episode of *Star Trek: The Next Generation*. And thus, Mae Jemison also has the distinction of being the first real astronaut to appear on the television series.

TONI MORRISON

THE FIRST BLACK WOMAN TO WIN
THE NOBEL PRIZE IN LITERATURE (1993)

"

*If there's a book you want to read,
but it hasn't been written yet, then you must write it.*

"

Toni Morrison's childhood in Ohio was surrounded by stories—fables and ghost tales, as well as firsthand accounts of life in the American South. Her parents used storytelling as a way to prepare their children for the world. These tales "were pretty much horror stories about life as an African American," she recalled later in life.

Toni also loved to read, especially Jane Austen and Russian author Leo Tolstoy. However, she couldn't help feeling that most books were meant for white readers. She strove to change that as an adult, when she became an editor at a publishing company in New York City. Toni worked hard to make sure black stories got published as well. Eventually, she picked up the pen and began writing her own books.

Toni's debut novel, *The Bluest Eye*, came out in 1970 and gained the attention of critics and readers who were moved by her depictions of the African American experience. She often writes about characters who must learn to cope with an unjust society. In her best-known work, *Beloved*, a mother is forced to make an impossible choice to spare her child from slavery.

In 1993, Toni was awarded the Nobel Prize in Literature for her work, the first black woman to win the prestigious award. "I'm writing for black people," she said in an interview, "in the same way that Tolstoy was not writing for me, a fourteen-year-old colored girl from Lorain, Ohio."

JOHN HERRINGTON

THE FIRST NATIVE AMERICAN IN SPACE (2002)

Like many children in the 1960s, John Herrington worshiped the real-life astronauts he saw on television. He would jump into a cardboard box and pretend it was a rocket that would fly him to the moon.

Born in Oklahoma as a member of the Chickasaw Nation, John adored nature and the outdoors. When he went to college, he thought he might become a forest ranger. However, John spent more time outdoors than reading. He dropped out due to poor grades.

To earn money, John began working on a survey team in Colorado. The state was widening a highway and needed someone to rappel down the cliff faces to take measurements. There, hanging off a canyon wall and calculating distances, John discovered that he really enjoyed math. He returned to college at the University of Colorado.

John had not forgotten his childhood dream of reaching space. After graduating with a degree in applied math, John joined the US Navy as a pilot and engineer, logging over 3,800 flight hours in over thirty different types of aircraft. In 1996, NASA selected him as an astronaut for the sixteenth shuttle mission to visit the International Space Station.

Having found his path on his own terms, John became not only the first Native American in space but also the first to walk there. He honored his heritage during that first space walk by carrying the Chickasaw Nation's flag, six eagle feathers, two arrowheads, and a braid of sweetgrass.

"

Each of us . . .
NEEDS TO BE A
MENTOR
for those that come
BEHIND US.

BE THE GUIDE

SHINING A LIGHT

DOWN A DARK AND

confusing path.

"

—JOHN HERRINGTON

ZAHA HADID

THE FIRST WOMAN TO RECEIVE THE PRITZKER ARCHITECTURE PRIZE (2004)

"

There are

360

DEGREES,

SO WHY STICK TO ONE?

"

Born in Iraq in 1950, Zaha Hadid grew up feeling like she had limitless potential, thanks largely to her parents' progressive thinking. Her father was the head of a political party dedicated to improving democracy in Iraq. Her mother was an artist. "My parents instilled in me a passion for discovery," she has said. Zaha's mother let her do the interior design for a guest room, inspiring a passion for creating spaces. And after studying mathematics in college, Zaha decided to go to architecture school in London.

Zaha's creative approach to design quickly drew praise but also raised some eyebrows. Her buildings were fluid and abstract, avoiding typical ninety-degree angles. Her former professor Rem Koolhaas once described Zaha as "a planet in her own inimitable orbit."

While she won awards for her avant-garde designs, she had a hard time getting anyone to actually build them—Zaha began to be known as a "paper architect." But Zaha stuck with it, never compromising her vision.

Finally, her design for the Vitra Fire Station in Weil am Rhein, Germany, was built, with construction finishing in 1993. She was forty-three years old. Once people saw how wonderful the building looked in real life, they clamored for more.

Zaha became a highly sought-after architect, especially after her innovative design in 2003 for the Lois & Richard Rosenthal Center for Contemporary Art in Cincinnati, Ohio. It was the first American museum designed by a woman. Zaha went on to design more than 950 buildings in forty-four countries. In 2004, she was the first woman to receive the most prestigious award in architecture, the Pritzker Architecture Prize, for her body of work.

JENNIFER YUH NELSON

THE FIRST WOMAN TO SOLELY DIRECT
AN ANIMATED FEATURE FROM A
MAJOR HOLLYWOOD STUDIO (2011)

"

WHEN YOU MAKE A MOVIE,

it's just so personal

AND THEN YOU PUT IT OUT IN FRONT OF PEOPLE AND IT BECOMES

something else.

"

As a young girl in California, Jennifer Yuh Nelson would sit at the kitchen table for hours, drawing with her mother and older sisters around a table. "Any piece of paper around the house was always covered in drawings," Jennifer has said in interviews.

Jennifer followed her sisters to California State University, where she got a degree in illustration. And like her sisters, Jennifer pursued a career in animation. After first working as a storyboard artist on the animated TV show *The Real Adventures of Jonny Quest*, Jennifer moved over to movies and joined DreamWorks Animation in 1998.

When the film *Kung Fu Panda* went into production, Jennifer was given the opportunity to direct the opening scene, which featured a beautiful 2-D action sequence. Later on, when it came time to pick a director for the sequel, producer Melissa Cobb approached Jennifer for the job.

At first, Jennifer thought she was too quiet and inexperienced to be a director, but she also felt encouraged by the producer's faith in her abilities. "She said, 'You can do it. You have done it. That whole thing with the opening sequence was a test, and you passed.'"

With *Kung Fu Panda 2*, Jennifer became the first woman to direct a feature-length animated film from a major studio. The movie went on to earn $665 million and earned an Academy Award nomination for Best Animated Feature Film. And until 2017's *Wonder Woman*, it was the highest-grossing film directed by a woman—ever.

MINDY KALING

When Mindy Kaling's parents were about to move to America, they wanted to pick an American name for their yet-to-be-born daughter. After watching the sitcom *Mork & Mindy*, they landed on the name Mindy. As fate would have it, Mindy Kaling would one day become a TV sensation in her own right.

Growing up in Cambridge, Massachusetts, Mindy seemed a quiet and studious wallflower. However, her personality bloomed in the jokes and stories that she would write. In high school, she decided she would write plays for a living. Her parents were supportive of her career path, and Mindy graduated from Dartmouth College with a playwriting degree in 2001.

She got her first taste of success when she cowrote and starred in a satirical play called *Matt and Ben*, a spoof about actors Ben Affleck and Matt Damon. The play helped land her a writing job on the television show *The Office*. Mindy was twenty-four years old (and the only woman) when she joined the show's writing team. Eventually, she went on to act on the series and even directed some episodes.

When *The Office* ended, Mindy decided to develop a sitcom about a complex, relatable character, the type of role not often offered to women of color. "The thing I'm most excited about with the show is to watch it stand the test of time and see young women—particularly young women of color—watch the show in five years and see she didn't have to be perfect," Mindy has said.

With the debut of *The Mindy Project* in the fall of 2012, Mindy made history as the first Indian American to star in a television show.

"

IT'S IMPORTANT FOR ME TO BE someone PEOPLE LOOK UP TO—most directly,

MINORITY GIRLS

who want to

DO WHAT I DO.

"

— MINDY KALING

MARISSA MAYER

THE FIRST WOMAN TO TOP *FORTUNE*'S 40 UNDER 40 LIST (2013)

"
*I always did something I was a little not ready to do.
I think that's how you grow.*
"

Marissa Ann Mayer's knack for juggling multiple ambitions came early. Her childhood in Wisconsin was filled to the brim with after-school activities. She took ballet lessons, went ice skating, joined Girl Scouts, and participated on the debate team. The daughter of an engineer and an art teacher, Marissa also had a gift for numbers. While working at a grocery store in high school, she would memorize the codes for vegetable produce in order to make the checkout process faster.

Marissa thought she might pursue a medical degree when she started college. But while at Stanford University, she discovered a passion for computers when she took an introductory course her freshman year. After she graduated with a master's degree in computer science, Marissa joined a newly established company called Google in 1999. She became their twentieth employee and first female engineer.

Back then, Google was not the technology giant it is today. Marissa's work at Google involved launching some of the company's most iconic and successful products, including Google Maps, Google News, and Gmail. With an eye for design, Marissa helped shape the unique look and feel of Google. She became one of the most sought-after leaders in the tech industry, eventually moving over to Yahoo! as its CEO in 2012.

In 2013, she made history by becoming the first woman to reach number one on *Fortune* magazine's list of the top forty business stars under forty years old. That September, Marissa also became the first CEO of a Fortune 500 company to be featured in a *Vogue* magazine fashion spread.

MARYAM MIRZAKHANI

THE FIRST WOMAN TO WIN THE FIELDS MEDAL (2014)

> "
> *The beauty of mathematics only shows itself to more patient followers.*
> "

As a young girl during the end of the Iran-Iraq war, Iranian-born Maryam Mirzakhani thought she would become a writer. Her favorite pastimes were exploring bookstores and reading novels. Though she would become one of the most esteemed mathematicians in the world, she actually struggled with at least one math class in middle school. It wasn't until her last year in high school, with ongoing encouragement from her brother, that she discovered the types of math that would spark her interest. "The more I spent time on maths, the more excited I got," she recalled in an interview.

By the time she graduated from university, Maryam was a highly decorated student, having won gold medals and earned a perfect score in the International Mathematical Olympiad as the first female ever named to Iran's team. At Harvard, she began to specialize in dynamic mathematics, which deals with the physics of motion and how they change over time.

Many of the formulas Maryam worked on were very advanced. For example, she often dealt with hyperbolic spaces—complex geometric structures that do not contain end points. Her work on how dynamic math could be applied to geometry earned her the prestigious Fields Medal in 2014. She was the first woman to win the award, considered the highest honor in mathematics.

TU YOUYOU

THE FIRST CHINESE WOMAN TO WIN A NOBEL PRIZE (2015)

"

It is my dream that Chinese medicine will help us conquer life-threatening diseases worldwide.

"

Raised on the eastern coast of China during the 1930s and '40s, Tu Youyou was no stranger to disease and war. She grew up during the Second Sino-Japanese War (which took place from 1937 to 1945), and she missed two years of high school because she contracted tuberculosis. Her long battle with the disease inspired her to study medicine at the Peking University in Beijing.

In the 1960s, China's leader Mao Zedong secretly set out to find a cure for malaria, a life-threatening disease that is transferred by mosquitoes to humans. North Vietnam had sought China's help in fighting the disease during its war against the United States. Youyou was assigned to look for a treatment in traditional Chinese medicines.

Youyou and her team combed through medical literature and folk recipes and tested hundreds of herbal extracts for

clues. One extract, from the herb *Artemisia annua*, appeared to kill the parasites that cause malaria, but it did not always work. Youyou studied the original text closer.

Her team had extracted the compound with boiling water, but Youyou found that the original recipe had not mentioned heating. She wondered whether the high temperature killed the active ingredient. She devised different methods of extraction at lower temperatures that involved water, ethanol, and ethyl ether. The extract with ethyl ether proved 100 percent effective, and the resulting drugs from the artemisinin compound have led to the survival and improved health of millions of people.

In 2015, she was awarded the Nobel Prize in Physiology or Medicine, making her the first Chinese woman to win the international award.

AVA DUVERNAY

THE FIRST AFRICAN AMERICAN WOMAN TO DIRECT A FILM NOMINATED FOR THE ACADEMY AWARD FOR BEST PICTURE (2015)

> "
> *If your dream is only about you, it's too small.*
> "

During her summer vacations, Ava DuVernay would visit the childhood home of her stepfather in Alabama, not far from the town of Selma. In 1965, African Americans, led by Dr. Martin Luther King Jr., began the march for civil rights there. King and his supporters were met with police brutality, but the media attention ultimately pressured President Lyndon Johnson into signing the Voting Rights Act later that year. Ava's stepfather told her about how he witnessed the marches first-hand as a child. As Ava listened, she thought about how stories like her stepfather's made history feel more human.

As an adult, Ava began a career in Hollywood, helping promote other people's movies. Over time, she thought about the stories that she wanted to see that were not being made into movies. One day, she decided she would make them herself.

"For me to pick up a camera as a black woman who did not go to film school— this is a testament to whatever path you're on right now is not necessarily the path you have to stay on," Ava has said.

After each of her projects wrapped up, more people took notice of her talent. Today, Ava has accomplished many firsts, including becoming the first black woman to lead a feature film with a budget of over $100 million. In 2015, she was also the first African American woman to direct a film nominated for a Best Picture Academy Award. It was the first major film about Martin Luther King Jr. and his fellow activists. That movie was called *Selma*.

RIZ AHMED

THE FIRST MAN OF ASIAN DESCENT TO WIN
AN EMMY AWARD FOR ACTING (2017)

The son of Pakistani immigrants who migrated to London, Riz Ahmed grew up trying to find his place between two cultures. At eleven years old, he was granted a scholarship to attend Merchant Taylors' School, a prestigious prep school for boys. Coming from a different background than the school's previous students, Riz disliked learning about world history from only one point of view—that of the Western colonizers.

He became passionate about issues of cultural identity and minority representation in media. After graduating from Oxford University, Riz dove headfirst into acting. He wanted to show what true diversity of perspectives should look like. "I never thought acting would be a realistic job for me," he said. "Because, quite frankly, I didn't see people who looked like me doing it. I quickly realized, that's all the more reason to try."

After various supporting roles, Riz landed the lead in the HBO miniseries *The Night Of.* He played a Pakistani American college student accused of murder. The show examined the tragic effects of the criminal justice system on his character, Nasir Khan. "I really believe that we all contain the potential to be anyone in a different set of circumstances," Riz said about his story arc.

Riz's powerful performance garnered tons of acclaim, including the Emmy Award for Outstanding Lead Actor in a Limited Series or Movie, making him the first man of Asian descent to win an Emmy acting award.

"

Representation
IS ABSOLUTELY
FUNDAMENTAL
in terms of what we
EXPECT FROM OUR
CULTURE,
and from our politics.

WE ALL WANT TO FEEL
REPRESENTED.
We want to
FEEL SEEN
AND HEARD
and valued.

"

—RIZ AHMED

JOHANNA LUCHT

THE FIRST DEAF ENGINEER IN AN ACTIVE CREWED MISSION CONTROL ROLE AT NASA (2017)

"

I JUST PROVED THAT A **DEAF PERSON** *can participate in a control room* DURING A MANNED AERONAUTICS MISSION, *so why not a deaf* ASTRONAUT IN SPACE?

"

Johanna Lucht had a hard time in school as a child. Her school in Germany lacked resources for deaf children, making it difficult for Johanna to learn to read and to communicate with her classmates. Finally, when she turned nine years old, an interpreter was brought in to teach her American Sign Language.

Over the next few months, Johanna's world opened up. She could carry on full conversations for the first time in ASL. Johanna transformed from a struggling, discouraged student to one who graduated high school with top honors.

Since Johanna was able to hone her math skills before her language ones, she found that she excelled in the subject. She decided to study computer science at the University of Minnesota after participating in a summer program that encouraged deaf students to study STEM. One day during her junior year of college, she received an email about a NASA internship. She didn't apply right away, thinking it would be too much of a long shot. Finally, after she received a third email, Johanna applied.

She was shocked when she was accepted. "I pinched myself, and decided this was really happening," she said. Johanna proved herself to be an excellent worker, and after her internship was over, she was offered a job.

Johanna was the first deaf engineer to help manage a crewed NASA flight from mission control. With an interpreter, she seamlessly worked with hearing engineers in a fast-paced environment, interpreting live data from the aircraft. Her advice for aspiring deaf scientists and engineers? "Never give up," she says. "When you have patience and take time to educate those who are willing to listen, you will gain hearing allies."

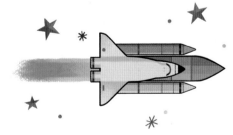

What will YOU BE THE FIRST TO DO?

WHO DID IT FIRST?
ACROSS TIME

 MARY GOLDA ROSS 1942

 MERET OPPENHEIM 1936

 ROBERT H. GODDARD 1926

 NETTIE STEVENS 1905

 BARNUM BROWN 1902

 HEDY LAMARR 1942

 MARGUERITE THOMAS WILLIAMS 1942

 CLAUDE SHANNON 1948

 MARIA TALLCHIEF 1949

 ALAN TURING 1950

 ELLEN OCHOA 1993

 TONI MORRISON 1993

 MAE JEMISON 1992

 ANTONIA NOVELLO 1990

 SYLVIA EARLE 1990

TIMOTHY BERNERS-LEE 1989

 JOHN HERRINGTON 2002

 ZAHA HADID 2004

 KATHRYN BIGELOW 2010

 JENNIFER YUH NELSON 2011

 MINDY KALING 2012

 MARISSA MAYER 2013

A long time ago

 ISAAC NEWTON 1668

 MARIA GAETANA AGNESI 1748

 CAROLINE HERSCHEL 1782

 ADA LOVELACE 1843

 NIKOLA TESLA 1887

 CHARLES FRITTS 1883

 EMILY WARREN ROEBLING 1883

 ELLEN SWALLOW RICHARDS 1870

 MARIA MITCHELL 1865

 ELIZABETH BLACKWELL 1849

 JAMES E. M. WEST 1962

 JANE GOODALL 1963

 MARY ALLEN WILKES 1964

 TEMPLE GRANDIN 1965

 MARY KENNETH KELLER 1965

 RALPH BAER 1972

 LONNIE G. JOHNSON 1989

 DEBBIE GIBSON 1988

 ARETHA FRANKLIN 1987

 THAI LEE 1985

 ALEXA CANADY 1981

 WALTER ALVAREZ 1980

 MARYAM MIRZAKHANI 2014

 MEGAN SMITH 2014

 TU YOUYOU 2015

 AVA DUVERNAY 2015

 RIZ AHMED 2017

 JOHANNA LUCHT 2017

Time will tell!

ILLUSTRATOR'S NOTE

The process for making the illustrations for *Who Did It First?* began with research (as it does for all of my work). I wanted to know as much as I could about each person's life story, their achievements, and their unique contribution to history so that I could capture their essence visually. Of course, I looked at photographs and images of each subject featured in the book, but I also searched for images to inspire me. So, for example, when creating the illustration of

Sylvia Earle, I not only looked at pictures of Sylvia, but I also pored over photos, paintings, and designs of fish. And that led me to search for images of all kinds of undersea life to see if anything might spark my imagination to make the illustration more fun and unexpected.

Once I completed my research, I was ready to go! For each portrait, the process was the same: I start with a rough sketch in pencil.

Next, I make a much more detailed sketch on the computer, which I will end up using in the finished illustration.

I always make a color plan before I add any color to my image, which means I pick around five or six shades that will help create the mood I'm aiming for. For Sylvia, I wanted to create

an underwater scene that was bright and sunny, and even a little magical with the whimsical coral designs and geometric fish so I used this palette:

I add color by painting digitally in the computer using a monitor called a CINTIQ that I can draw on directly, and the design program I use is called Photoshop. I layer colors on top of each other using different brushes created for Photoshop, just like using real brushes and paint! Once I'm done painting, I add special digital textures for that final extra touch.

— CAITLIN KUHWALD

FURTHER EXPLORATION

There's much more to the amazing pioneers featured in this book than could possibly fit within. Here are some additional reading and resources to help you learn more:

BOOKS

Carlson, W. Bernard. *Tesla: Inventor of the Electrical Age*. Princeton, New Jersey: Princeton University Press, 2013.

Clary, David A. *Rocket Man: Robert H. Goddard and the Birth of the Space Age*. New York: Theia, 2003.

Dingus, Lowell. *Barnum Brown: The Man Who Discovered* Tyrannosaurus rex. Berkeley, California: University of California Press, 2010.

Dougherty, Rachel. *Secret Engineer: How Emily Roebling Built the Brooklyn Bridge*. New York: Roaring Brook Press, 2019.

Essinger, James. *Ada's Algorithm: How Lord Byron's Daughter Ada Lovelace Launched the Digital Age*. Brooklyn, New York: Melville House, 2014.

Gormley, Beatrice. *Maria Mitchell: The Soul of an Astronomer*. Grand Rapids, Michigan: Eerdmans Books for Young Readers, 2004.

Hadid, Zaha, and Aaron Betsky. *Zaha Hadid: The Complete Buildings and Projects*. New York: Rizzoli, 1998.

Kaling, Mindy. *Why Not Me?* New York: Crown Archetype, 2015.

Li, Stephanie. *Toni Morrison: A Biography*. Santa Barbara, California: Greenwood Press, 2009.

Medina, Nico. *Who Is Aretha Franklin?* New York: Penguin Workshop, an imprint of Penguin Random House, 2018.

Nivola, Claire A. *Life in the Ocean: The Story of Oceanographer Sylvia Earle*. New York: Frances Foster Books, Farrar Straus Giroux, 2012.

Ottaviani, Jim. *Primates: The Fearless Science of Jane Goodall, Dian Fossey, and Biruté Galdikas*. New York: First Second, 2013.

Peterson, Dale. *Jane Goodall: The Woman Who Redefined Man*. Boston: Houghton Mifflin Co., 2006.

Schwartz, Heather E. *Code-breaker and Mathematician Alan Turing*. Minneapolis: Lerner Publications, 2018.

Shepherd, Jodie. *Mae Jemison*. New York: Children's Press, an imprint of Scholastic Inc., 2015.

Soni, Jimmy. *A Mind at Play: How Claude Shannon Invented the Information Age*. New York: Simon & Schuster, 2017.

Stone, Tanya Lee. *Who Says Women Can't Be Computer Programmers?* New York: Henry Holt Books for Young Readers, 2018.

Tallchief, Maria, and Rosemary Wells. *Tallchief: America's Prima Ballerina*. New York: Puffin Books, 1999.

WEBSITES

http://www.avaduvernay.com/

Time Magazine's Firsts: Women Who Are Changing the World: http://time.com/collection/firsts/4921998/firsts-full-list

VIDEOS & DOCUMENTARIES

Chickasaw.TV, Interview with John Herrington, Season 1, Episode 1, 2017: https://www.chickasaw.tv/

DigiBarnTV, Interview with Mary Allen Wilkes, 2011: https://youtu.be/Cmv6p8hN0xQ

Dean, Alexandra, dir. *Bombshell: The Hedy Lamarr Story*, 2017.

ALEX HART is the pseudonym for a children's book editor and author who is the first person in his family to write and publish a book. He lives with his husband in Brooklyn, New York, and Hillsdale, New York.

JULIE LEUNG works in book publishing as a marketing director by day. By night, she writes and writes. She is the author of the Mice of the Round Table series and *Paper Son: The Story of Tyrus Wong*. She lives in Brooklyn, New York, with her husband, and is the first person to win a game of Lord of the Rings Trivial Pursuit against him.

JLEUNGBOOKS.COM

CAITLIN KUHWALD has a BFA in illustration from the California College of the Arts in San Francisco and an MFA in painting from the Pennsylvania Academy of the Fine Arts. Her work has appeared in various magazines, books, and even on DVD covers. Additionally, Caitlin teaches illustration at the University of California–San Diego. *Who Did It First? 50 Scientists, Artists, and Mathematicians Who Revolutionized the World* is her first book for children. She lives in Los Angeles, California.

CAITLINKUHWALD.COM

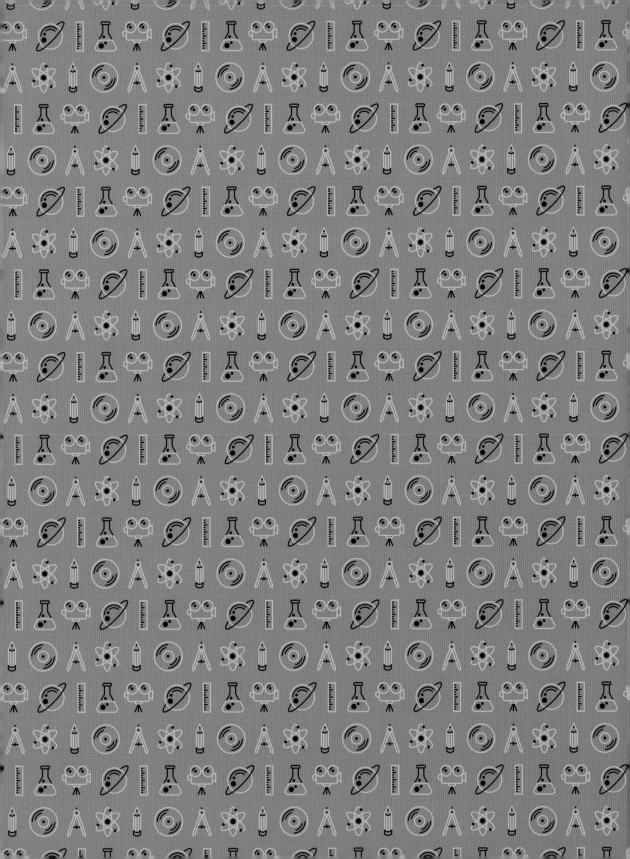

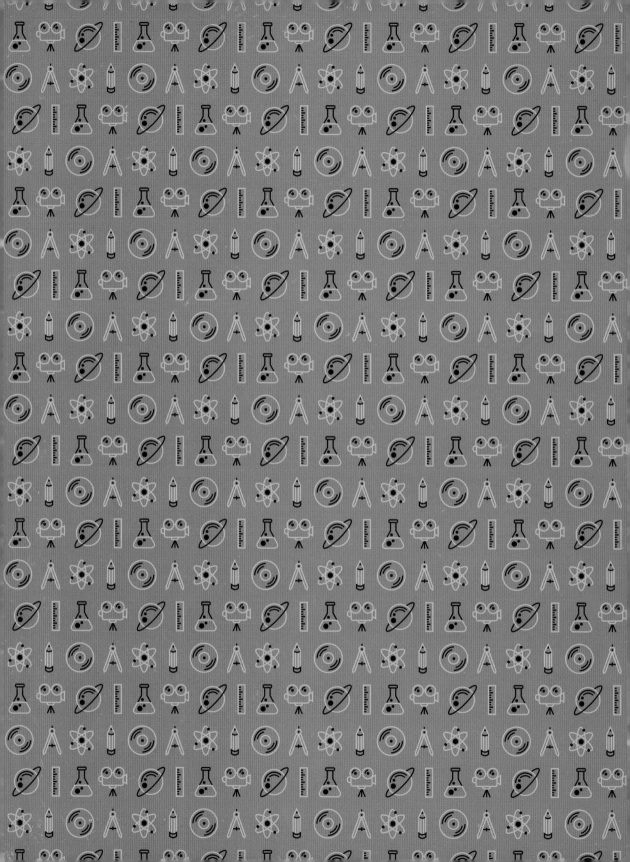